Robert Burns
for Beginners

Robert Burns
for Beginners

Rennie McOwan

First published in 1995 by
SAINT ANDREW PRESS
121 George Street, Edinburgh EH2 4YN.

Copyright © Rennie McOwan 1995

ISBN 0 7152 0715 6

British Library Cataloguing in Publication Data
A catalogue record for this book
is available from the British Library.

ISBN 0715207156

Cover design and **internal layout** by Mark Blackadder.
Cover photographs by Walter Bell.
Typesetting in Helvetica and Bembo by Lesley Ann Taylor.
Printed and **bound** in Great Britain by Bell & Bain Ltd, Glasgow.

Contents

For
MONICA GORDON
A Good Friend and Dedicated Teacher

Dedication

SPECIAL thanks are due to SUSAN SMELT
of Milton of Campsie,
who in April 1994 won a
National Certificate of Merit for Excellence in Project Work
on ROBERT BURNS
presented by the BURNS FEDERATION
and who made helpful suggestions towards this book.

Thanks are also due to JIMMY BLACK
for his wise advice and encouragement;

to A. G. BARR p.l.c.
for their permission to use the product Irn-Bru®
on the cover of this book;

and to ALLOWAY PUBLISHING, Ayrshire
for their courtesy and help.

Acknowledgments

Happy Birthday
Robert Burns

JANUARY the 25th is a very special day. Why? Because one of the world's best-known poets was born on that day in 1759. This poet was born in Alloway, a little village in Ayrshire, Scotland.

What was the name of this poet? His name was *Robert Burns.*

Every year, in the month of January, people in many different countries remember Robert Burns. Why is that? Because the poems and songs of this man from Alloway are so popular that they have been translated into many languages. For example, one of his songs – 'Auld Lang Syne' – is sung all over the world when people want to remember being happy together. They sing it just before they have to say good-bye and leave each other.

Lines and verses from poems by Robert Burns are admired and remembered by people all over the world. They are often repeated by other writers – in books, plays, scripts for radio and television, and so on. These verses are called 'quotations', and these quotations are often used by famous men and women when making great public speeches.

People use these 'quotations' because Robert's verses are so clever and well-written. They use them because the words mean a lot to them. The words can make them happy or sad. Perhaps they want to say something important or funny or special – and they cannot find quite the right words to say it for themselves – and, anyway, they know that Robert Burns said it better than they ever could.

So they think he's brilliant! They really enjoy his poems and sometimes learn them off by heart. Yes, they remember Robert Burns and they honour him.

What are Robert's poems like? Well, some are long. Some are short. Some are in the English language. Some are in Scots. Some are in both. When reading his poems, you will know most of the words he uses, but if you don't, you can always ask someone – like your teacher, your mother or father, or a friend, or someone at your local library.

We are very lucky in Scotland because we have three beautiful languages.

The first is *Gaelic*, a language spoken in many parts of Scotland long ago. Today it is mainly spoken in parts of the Highlands and Islands. Robert Burns could not speak Gaelic, but he knew it was an important language and he respected it.

The second is *Scots*. It is not spoken all the time these days, but most Scottish people know lots of Scots words. They are very rich words. They are strong words. They are colourful words. People in country areas, towns and villages still use Scots words. We should be proud of these words. They are part of our Scottish heritage. It is good to know these words.

You might have friends who live in another city, town or village. Have you ever noticed that some of the words they say *sound* different to the way that you say them? And they will think that you sound different to them. These differences are called 'accents'. For example, the word 'fish' is pronounced 'fush' or 'feesh' in different parts of the country. Or – another example – the word 'no' is pronounced 'nae' ('nay') or sometimes 'na'. Can you think of any other words like this?

Sometimes, in different parts of Scotland, we use a different word to mean the same thing – for example, the words 'chiel' and 'loon' both mean a 'lad' or 'fellow'; and 'quean' and 'lass' mean a 'young woman'. These words are part of our local dialect.

Another example – a 'forkie-tail' and a 'clipshear' are the same thing. Find out what this is by looking up a dictionary of the Scots language. In which areas of Scotland are these words used?

Lots of these words, even those still used today, were once part of the old Scots language. It is good that they are still used in some form or other. They are, after all, part of our heritage in Scotland. Try to use them if you can.

Robert Burns certainly loved Scots words and the Scots language. His poetry is full of Scots words.

The third language used in Scotland is modern *English*. Robert Burns wrote in that language as well. Today nearly all of us speak in modern English. Television uses modern English. It too is a beautiful language.

So, remember – Robert Burns liked *Gaelic*. He liked *English*. But most of all he liked the *Scots* language. It was the language of the people of his time and it is still around in many ways in the language we speak and use today in Scotland.

★　★　★

[The format of this book has been designed in such a way as to help the reader understand the main aspects of a Burns Supper. Thus he or she should be able easily to understand the background and programme of the Supper and be encouraged to organise one for themselves at home or in school.

Questions, Things To Do and Follow-up Exercises are a feature of this book. In addition, useful reference books are noted on page 87 to assist you in your fact-finding searches.]

Robb

CHAPTER 1

Who is
Robert Burns?

ROBERT

Burns' mother and father were not rich people. They had a small house in Alloway, Ayrshire, which Robert's father, William, built himself. William (1721-84) worked as gardener to Provost Ferguson. Before this, William Burns (or 'Burnes' as it was often spelt) was recorded as a tenant-farmer of Alloway when he married Agnes Broun (1732-1820) of Craigenton, Maybole.

Their son Robert was born on the 25th of January 1759. In 1766, while the poet-to-be was still a young boy, William rented a farm at Mount Oliphant, near Alloway. This can still be seen today.

Robert did not go to school like you do. William and other farmers in the area paid money to hire a teacher for their children. Robert liked reading best. This helped him to become a great poet later on.

Robert and his brothers worked very hard on their parent's farm, even as small children. Some people think Robert worked a bit too hard on the farm. He was often out in the cold and rain and the work was back-breaking. This may be part of the reason why he became ill with angina, heart trouble and rheumatic fever in later life.

The Burns family moved again in 1777 — this time to another farm called Lochlea (also spelt 'Lochlie'), in Tarbolton, also in Ayrshire. Sadly, the family found farm life very difficult there.

But things were not all bad. When Robert was in his twenties he and his friends formed a club where they could meet together socially from time to time. They met in Tarbolton and spent the evenings arguing with one another, learning to dance and talking about girls. The club, called the 'Tarbolton Bachelors' Club', was for men and boys only. (A 'bachelor' is an unmarried man.) Do you think a club *just* for men and boys is fair? It was the fashion then. Women and girls were not allowed to become members. If you visit Tarbolton, you can still see the building where the club was held.

As Robert grew up, he began to write poems for girls he liked. But he began to write other poems as well. Sometimes he wrote words to match tunes that people already knew.

Robert was only 25 years old when his father died. The family moved to another farm after that. It was called Mossgiel, near Mauchline, in Ayrshire.

By this time Robert was a popular man with the ladies. He had lots of girlfriends and some people didn't like him for it. They thought he was selfish. They thought he was too keen on noisy parties and drinking. They thought he was not a very kind person.

When some Church people criticised him, Robert became angry with the Church itself. He thought these people were being too narrow-minded. So he criticised them back, sometimes in his poems. 'Holy Willie's Prayer' is a good example of this.

In 1786 a book of poems by Robert Burns was published. People read it and told others to read it and soon lots of men and women were reading it. He became famous – *everyone* was reading the poems of Robert Burns!

So off Robert went to Scotland's capital city, Edinburgh, where important people went out their way to meet him – publishers, printers, lawyers and titled people like the Marquis of Graham, the Duke of Portland and the Duke of Montague.

Robert also took time to visit other parts of Scotland, including the Highlands. He loved the beautiful, sweeping landscapes there.

A second book of poems was published on the 31st of July 1786. Like the last volume, the new book became very popular. Robert was now becoming as well known to everyone then as a film star or pop singer or famous footballer is today.

As we said earlier, Robert Burns liked girls – but he wasn't always very kind to them. He often managed to get himself into a lot of trouble with their parents and friends, who thought he was a bad and selfish man. But Robert could also be gentle. He could be thoughtful. Some of the beautiful love songs and poems he wrote are now famous all over the world.

Burns eventually married a girl called Jean Armour and they had children. He rented a farm called Ellisland, near Dumfries and built a house for his growing family.

Robert needed more money. A family can cost a lot of money in food and clothes. So he found himself another job. He became an Exciseman, like a modern-day Customs Officer. His job was to stop people smuggling goods and trying to make whisky in secret to avoid paying a government tax called 'duty'. Because of the type of work an Exciseman had to do – laying down the Law – it was not a popular job. Robert wrote a poem/song about this called 'The Deil's awa wi th' Exciseman'. It tells how the Devil had taken the Exciseman away – and lots of people were very glad to hear about this.

At the same time Robert kept working on his farm. It was a hard life. No wonder he became very ill and had to give up the farm.

Robert had to work very hard at his job as an Exciseman. He had to travel a lot on horseback and it was very tiring. His health really suffered. So doctors packed him off to the Solway Firth for a spot of sea bathing – they thought it would help to cure his illness. We know nowadays that this was not a wise thing to do – in fact, it only made matters worse.

Robert and his wife Jean had more children, but sadly Robert was not destined to live much longer. He died on the 21st of July 1796. He was only 37 years old.

However, the poems and songs of Robert Burns live on. Let us now look at some of them.

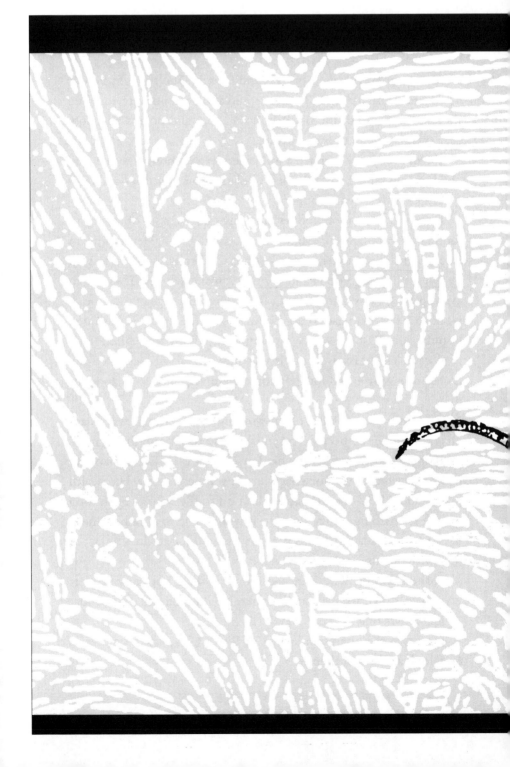

CHAPTER 2

Robert Burns
and the Mouse

MORE and more books of Robert's poems were published after his death, until he became well known all over the world. Robert wrote all kinds of poems. He wrote sad poems and joyful poems. He loved the countryside and wrote about small things like mice or daisies. He wanted everyone to enjoy a good life and not to be hungry or poor or feel threatened. Instead they should have dignity and freedom. He loved Scotland and praised this country in his poems and songs. These were the subjects that interested him.

On the next page you will find a famous Burns short poem called 'To a Mouse'. This is how it came to be written. One day, when Robert was out in the fields ploughing, the blade of his plough – the plough-blade was known as a 'coulter' – cut into the nest or den of a mouse. Robert was very sorry to have disturbed or hurt the mouse inside and this is a poem about his feelings. [There may be some puzzling words in this poem, but the meanings will be explained at the end of the poem.]

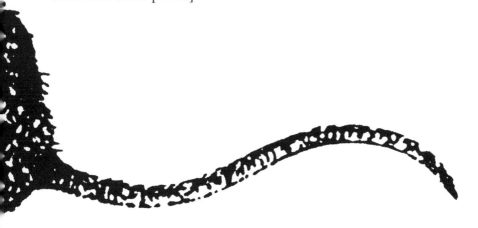

To a Mouse

ON TURNING HER UP IN HER NEST WITH THE PLOUGH
~ NOVEMBER 1785 ~

WEE sleekit, cow'rin, tim'rous beastie,
O, what a panic's in thy breastie!
Thou need na start awa sae hasty,
   Wi bickering brattle!
I wad be laith to rin an chase thee,
   Wi murdering pattle!

I'm truly sorry man's dominion
Has broken Nature's social union,
An justifies that ill opinion,
   Which makes thee startle
At me, thy poor, earth-born companion,
   An fellow mortal!

I doubt na, whyles, but thou may thieve;
What then? poor beastie, thou maun live!
A daimen icker in a thrave
   'S a sma request;
I'll get a blessin wi the lave,
   An never miss't!

Thy wee-bit housie, too, in ruin!
Its silly wa's the win's are strewin!
An naething, now, to big a new ane,
   O foggage green!
An bleak December's win's ensuin,
   Baith snell an keen!

Thou saw the fields laid bare an waste,
An weary winter comin fast,
An cozie here, beneath the blast,
      Thou thought to dwell,
Till crash! the cruel coulter past
      Out thro thy cell.

That wee bit heap o leaves an stibble,
Has cost thee monie a weary nibble!
Now thou's turn'd out, for a' thy trouble,
      But house or hald,
To thole the winter's sleety dribble,
      An cranreuch cauld!

But Mousie, thou art no thy lane,
In proving foresight may be vain:
The best-laid schemes o mice an men
      Gang aft agley,
An lea'e us nought but grief an pain,
      For promis'd joy!

Still thou art blest, compar'd wi me!
The present only toucheth thee:
But och! I backward cast my e'e,
      On prospects drear!
An forward, tho I canna see,
      I guess an fear!

WORD LIST

sleekit	=	smooth or glossy-coated
bickering brattle	=	a hurrying scamper
laith	=	loth, reluctant, sorry to …
pattle	=	a plough-scraper
whyles	=	at times
maun	=	must
daimen icker in a thrave	=	an odd ear in 24 sheaves of corn or barley
lave	=	the rest, the remainder
foggage green	=	coarse grass
snell	=	bitter, severe
coulter	=	a plough-blade
thole	=	to endure
cranreuch cauld	=	hoar frost
gang aft agley	=	often go wrong

QUESTIONS

– Robert Burns didn't mean to hurt the little mouse.
  Why then do you think he was so upset?
– He calls the mouse a 'fellow mortal'. What does he mean?
– What does he mean by saying:
     'A daimen icker in a thrave / 'S a sma request'?
  Is he angry that the mouse has been eating his corn or barley?

★ ★ ★

– The poet says:
     'The best-laid schemes o mice an men / Gang aft agley.'
  What feeling is he sharing with the mouse?

★ ★ ★

– Do you think this is an important poem?
– Is the poet just feeling sorry that he has wrecked the mouse's
  home, or is he telling us something else too? What else might he
  be trying to say?
– Robert Burns wrote the poem 'To a Mouse' in November 1785.
  Why do you think it is still a popular poem today?

THINGS TO DO

- Why not draw a picture of Robert Burns ploughing?
  You could draw him, the plough and the mouse.
  You might draw the mouse looking up at him, and the coulter
  (blade) of the plough just before the mouse runs away.
- Do you know what a furrow is?
  Try drawing some furrows in a field.
- Why not make a model of Burns, the plough and the mouse?

FOLLOW-UP EXERCISE

– Robert Burns wrote another poem like 'To a Mouse' when he cut down a daisy with his plough. It is called 'To a Mountain Daisy'. He wrote this poem in April 1786. There are nine verses and here is the first one:

> Wee, modest, crimson-tippèd flow'r,
> Thou's met me in an evil hour;
> For I maun crush amang the stoure
> Thy slender stem:
> To spare thee now is past my pow'r,
> Thou bonie gem.

– Do you think Robert was sorry to destroy the daisy – even though it was an accident?
– Do you know what 'maun' means?
– Do you know what 'stoure' means?
– You might like to draw Robert Burns' plough cutting down the daisy, or make a model of this event.

CHAPTER 3

Tam o Shanter's
Big Adventure

ARE you afraid of witches? There was a man called Tam o Shanter who certainly was! He was out riding on his horse – a mare called Maggie (Meg for short) – when he saw a *lot* of witches. It happened at a place called Kirk-Alloway in Ayrshire, at a church which was thought by local people to be haunted ....

Tam only escaped because his horse could gallop *very* fast when she had to and because – as the story tells us – witches cannot cross running water, like a burn as it was in this story.

But even though Meg was fast, one of the witches got very very close and grabbed at the poor horse's tail, pulling most of the hair out. Some waterfalls are called the 'Grey Mare's Tail' after this part of the story, because falling water looks a bit like a horse's tail. Perhaps there is a 'Grey Mare's Tail' waterfall near you.

Robert wrote about this local story in a poem which he called 'Tam o Shanter'. This poem is quite frightening in places, but parts of it are very funny as well and it makes many grown-ups laugh. It is called an 'epic' poem – meaning that it is long and it has a hero in it – Tam!

'Tam o Shanter' is also a very famous poem and it is recited at special events each year called Burns Suppers. (You will find out about these Suppers on pages 53-85.) Some grown-ups learn this poem by heart. This is not easy because, as we have said, it *is* a long poem – a *very* long poem – but it always gets lots of applause and cheers when it is recited.

Here is a brief outline of the story of the poem:

Tam has been to market, but it is now late at night and he must think about going home. This is not as easy as it may seem, however, because Tam has drunk too much beer and whisky. His wife, Kate, always gets very angry with him for getting drunk and Tam knows that he'll be in a lot of trouble when he gets home.

Astride his grey mare Maggie, slowly plodding along the path, Tam approaches the church of Kirk-Alloway. There he is amazed – no, *shocked!* – to see a crowd of witches and warlocks dancing in the kirk-yard. (A 'warlock' is a male witch.) Even the Devil himself is there, playing the bagpipes!

One young witch is dancing so well that she catches Tam's eye. He roars with delight – 'Weel done, Cutty-sark!' ('Cutty-sark' means 'short shirt' or 'chemise').

Suddenly there is silence … the witches stop their dancing … they spot the slightly tipsy Tam and begin to chase him.

Tam spurs his horse and gallops for his life, escaping … but only just!

This is a great poem, full of lively images. Enjoy it!

Tam o Shanter
A Tale

Of Brownyis and of Bogillis full is this Buke.
~ GAWIN DOUGLAS ~

WHEN chapman billies leave the street,
And drouthy neebors, neebors meet;
As market-days are wearing late,
An folk begin to tak the gate;
While we sit bousing at the nappy,
An getting fou and unco happy,
We think na on the lang Scots miles,
The mosses, waters, slaps, and styles,
That lie between us and our hame,
Whare sits our sulky, sullen dame,
Gathering her brows like gathering storm,
Nursing her wrath to keep it warm.

This truth fand honest Tam o Shanter,
As he frae Ayr ae night did canter:
(Auld Ayr, whom ne'er a town surpasses,
For honest men and bonie lasses).

O Tam hadst thou but been sae wise,
As taen thy ain wife Kate's advice!
She tauld thee weel thou was a skellum,
A blethering, blustering, drunken blellum;
That frae November till October,
Ae market-day thou was nae sober;

That ilka melder wi the miller,
Thou sat as lang as thou had siller;
That ev'ry naig was ca'd a shoe on,
The smith and thee gat roarin fou on;
That at the Lord's house, even on Sunday,
Thou drank wi Kirkton Jean till Monday.
She prophesied that, late or soon,
Thou would be found, deep drown'd in Doon,
Or catch'd wi warlocks in the mirk,
By Alloway's auld, haunted kirk.

Ah, gentle dames, it gars me greet,
To think how monie counsels sweet,
How monie lengthen'd, sage advices
The husband frae the wife despises!

But to our tale: – Ae market-night,
Tam had got planted unco right,
Fast by an ingle, bleezing finely,
Wi reaming swats, that drank divinely;
And at his elbow, Souter Johnie,
His ancient, trusty, drouthy cronie:
Tam lo'ed him like a very brither;
They had been fou for weeks thegither.
The night drave on wi sangs and clatter;
And ay the ale was growing better:
The landlady and Tam grew gracious,
Wi secret favours, sweet and precious:
The Souter tauld his queerest stories;
The landlord's laugh was ready chorus:
The storm without might rair and rustle,
Tam did na mind the storm a whistle.

Care, mad to see a man sae happy,
E'en drown'd himsel amang the nappy.
As bees flee hame wi lades o treasure,
The minutes wing'd their way wi pleasure:
Kings may be blest but Tam was glorious,
O'er a' the ills o life victorious!

But pleasures are like poppies spread:
You seize the flow'r, its bloom is shed;
Or like the snow falls in the river,
A moment white – then melts for ever;
Or like the borealis race,
That flit ere you can point their place;
Or like the rainbow's lovely form
Evanishing amid the storm.
Nae man can tether time or tide,
The hour approaches Tam maun ride:
That hour o night's black arch the key-stane,
That dreary hour Tam mounts his beast in:
And sic a night he taks the road in,
As ne'er poor sinner was abroad in.

The wind blew as 'twad blawn its last;
The rattling showers rose on the blast;
The speedy gleams the darkness swallow'd;
Loud, deep, and lang the thunder bellow'd;
That night, a child might understand,
The Deil had business on his hand.

Weel mounted on his grey mare Meg,
A better never lifted leg,
Tam skelpit on thro dub and mire,

Despising wind, and rain, and fire;
Whiles holding fast his guid blue bonnet,
Whiles crooning o'er some auld Scots sonnet,
Whiles glow'ring round wi prudent cares,
Lest bogles catch him unawares:
Kirk-Alloway was drawing nigh,
Whare ghaists and houlets nightly cry.

By this time he was cross the ford,
Whare in the snaw the chapman smoor'd;
And past the birks and meikle stane,
Whare drunken Charlie brak's neck-bane;
And thro the whins, and by the cairn,
Whare hunters fand the murder'd bairn;
And near the thorn, aboon the well,
Whare Mungo's mither hang'd hersel.
Before him Doon pours all his floods;
The doubling storm roars thro the woods;
The lightnings flash from pole to pole,
Near and more near the thunders roll:
When, glimmering thro the groaning trees,
Kirk-Alloway seem'd in a bleeze,
Thro ilka bore the beams were glancing,
And loud resounded mirth and dancing.

Inspiring bold John Barleycorn,
What dangers thou canst make us scorn!
Wi tippenny, we fear nae evil;
Wi usquabae, we'll face the Devil!
The swats sae ream'd in Tammie's noddle,
Fair play, he car'd na deils a boddle.

But Maggie stood, right sair astonish'd,
Till, by the heel and hand admonish'd,
She ventur'd forward on the light;
And, wow! Tam saw an unco sight!

Warlocks and witches in a dance:
Nae cotillion, brent new frae France,
But hornpipes, jigs, strathspeys, and reels,
Put life and mettle in their heels.
A winnock-bunker in the east,
There sat Auld Nick, in shape o beast;
A tousie tyke, black, grim and large,
To gie them music was his charge:
He screw'd the pipes and gart them skirl,
Till roof and rafters a' did dirl.
Coffins stood round, like open presses,
That shaw'd the dead in their last dresses;
And, by some devilish cantraip sleight,
Each in its cauld hand held a light:
By which heroic Tam was able
To note upon the haly table,
A murderer's banes, in gibbet-airns;
Twa span-lang, wee, unchristen'd bairns;
A thief new-cutted frae a rape –
Wi his last gasp his gab did gape;
Five tomahawks, wi blude red-rusted.
Five scymitars, wi murder crusted;
A garter which a babe had strangled;
A knife a father's throat had mangled –
Whom his ain son o life bereft –
The grey-hairs yet stack to the heft;

Wi mair of horrible and awefu,
Which even to name wad be unlawfu.

As Tammie glowr'd, amaz'd and curious,
The mirth and fun grew fast and furious;
The piper loud and louder blew,
The dancers quick and quicker flew,
They reel'd, they set, they cross'd, they cleekit,
Till ilka carlin swat and reekit,
And coost her duddies to the wark,
And linket at it in her sark!

Now Tam, O Tam! had thae been queans,
A' plump and strapping in their teens!
Their sarks, instead o creeshie flannen,
Been snaw-white seventeen hunder linen! –
Thir breeks o mine, my only pair,
That ance were plush, o guid blue hair,
I wad hae gien them off my hurdies,
For ae blink o the bonie burdies!
But wither'd beldams, auld and droll,
Rigwoodie hags wad spean a foal,
Louping and flinging on a crummock,
I wonder did na turn thy stomach!

But Tam kend what was what fu brawlie:
There was ae winsome wench and wawlie,
That night enlisted in the core,
Lang after kend on Carrick shore
(For monie a beast to dead she shot,
An perish'd monie a bonie boat,

And shook baith meikle corn and bear,
And kept the country-side in fear).
Her cutty sark, o Paisley harn,
That while a lassie she had worn,
In longitude tho sorely scanty,
It was her best, and she was vauntie …
Ah! little kend thy reverend grannie,
That sark she coft for her wee Nannie,
Wi twa pund Scots ('twas a' her riches),
Wad ever grac'd a dance of witches!

But here my Muse her wing maun cour,
Sic flights are far beyond her power:
To sing how Nannie lap and flang
(A souple jade she was and strang),
And how Tam stood like ane bewitch'd,
And thought his very een enrich'd;
Even Satan glowr'd, and fidg'd fu fain,
And hotch'd and blew wi might and main:
Till first ae caper, syne anither,
Tam tint his reason a' thegither,
And roars out, 'Weel done, Cutty-sark!'
And in an instant all was dark:
And scarcely had he Maggie rallied,
When out the hellish legion sallied.

As bees bizz out wi angry fyke,
When plundering herds assail their byke;
As open pussie's mortal foes,
When, pop! she starts before their nose;
As eager runs the market-crowd,

When 'Catch the thief!' resounds aloud:
So Maggie runs, the witches follow,
Wi monie an eldritch skriech and hollow.

Ah, Tam! Ah, Tam! thou'll get thy fairin!
In hell they'll roast thee like a herrin!
In vain thy Kate awaits thy comin!
Kate soon will be a woefu woman!
Now, do thy speedy utmost, Meg,
And win the key-stane of the brig;
There, at them thou thy tail may toss,
A running stream they dare na cross!
But ere the key-stane she could make,
The fient a tail she had to shake;
For Nannie, far before the rest,
Hard upon noble Maggie prest,
And flew at Tam wi furious ettle;
But little wist she Maggie's mettle!
Ae spring brought off her master hale,
But left behind her ain grey tail:
The carlin claught her by the rump,
An left poor Maggie scarce a stump.

Now, wha this tale o truth shall read,
Ilk man, and mother's son, take heed:
Whene'er to drink you are inclin'd,
Or cutty sarks run in your mind,
Think! ye may buy the joys o'er dear:
Remember Tam o Shanter's mare.

WORD LIST

chapman billies	=	pedlars
drouthy neebors	=	thirsty neighbours
fou	=	drunk
nappy	=	ale
ae	=	one
skellum	=	a good-for-nothing, a rogue
blellum	=	a babbler
ilka melder	=	every corn-grinding
siller	=	money
naig	=	a small horse or pony
mirk	=	darkness
gars me greet	=	makes me weep
rair	=	to roar
maun	=	must
Deil	=	the Devil
skelpit	=	spanked
dub	=	puddle
houlet	=	owl
smoor'd	=	smothered
birks	=	birches
meikle	=	big
aboon	=	above
ilka bore	=	every chink or opening
tippenny	=	twopenny beer, weak ale

usquabae	=	whisky
noddle	=	brain
boddle	=	a Scottish copper coin
unco	=	wondrous
cotillion	=	a lively dance
brent	=	brand
mettle	=	spirit, courage
winnock-bunker	=	a window-seat
tousie tyke	=	a shaggy dog
gart them skirl	=	made them squeal
dirl	=	to ring
presses	=	cupboards
cantraip sleight	=	a magic device
airns	=	irons
rape	=	a rope
gab	=	mouth
cleekit	=	took hold of
carlin	=	an old woman, hag
swat and reekit	=	sweated and steamed
coost her duddies to the wark	=	stripped off her clothes
linket	=	danced
sark; cutty-sark	=	shirt or chemise; short shirt
queans	=	girls, young women
creeshie flannen	=	greasy flannel cloth
seventeen hunder linen	=	fine linen of a 1700 thread gauge

hurdies	=	bottom, rear
beldams	=	old women, hags
rigwoodie	=	withered, shrivelled
crummock	=	a cudgel
brawlie	=	well
wawlie	=	choice
core	=	crew, company
bear	=	barley
Paisley harn	=	coarse cloth
vauntie	=	proud-looking
coft	=	bought, purchased
cour	=	to curb
fu fain	=	most fondly
hotch'd	=	jerked
syne	=	then
tint	=	lost
fyke	=	fret
byke	=	a hive
pussie	=	a hare
eldritch skriech	=	strange or unearthly screech
fairin	=	just deserts
ettle	=	aim, intention
hale	=	whole
claught	=	clawed

QUESTIONS

- Are there any other words that you didn't understand in this poem? If so, ask someone what they mean. Try to use some of these words in a sentence.
- In the poem, Tam has a friend called Souter Johnie. Do you know what a 'souter' is?
- Look at a detailed map of Scotland. Can you find any waterfalls called the 'Grey Mare's Tail?'

THINGS TO DO

- Why don't you make a model of haunted Alloway Kirk and Tam on his horse, Maggie, being chased by the witches?
- Or you could draw the scene – the kirk-yard, the burn with the running water the witches cannot cross. You could draw Maggie losing her tail to the witches.
- Or, if you are part of a large class, each member could pick a character from the poem, draw it, colour it, cut it out and stick it on to a background like the one suggested above, to make a frieze for your classroom wall.
- Or why not dress up? One of you could be Tam, two people could be the horse, others could be the witches and warlocks. Remember, you will need to make a tail which can be pulled off quite easily.
- Many people in Scotland wore a blue bonnet long ago. It looked rather like a large beret. Why don't you make a Tam o Shanter bonnet?
- Make a concertina book of a small part of the poem 'Tam o Shanter'. Each page could show one line of the poem, plus a picture of the action.
- Sometimes, instead of learning the whole poem by heart, grown-ups form a group or team of four or five people to read the poem, bit by bit. The first person reads a section and then hands it over to the second person, and so on. You could try that.
- As you grow older you may like to learn *all* this poem off by heart!

a health to
a health to
that his
liberty
May tyrants
And wander

CHAPTER 4

Robert Burns
Quotations

May Liberty meet wi' success

THE poem 'Tam o Shanter' is a great favourite and it has been translated into lots of different languages. However, it is not the only Burns poem or song to have become famous the world over. In fact over the years people have used a few lines of Robert's poetry here, and a verse or two there, until these lines and verses have become very familiar to us. On page 3 we talked about these lines and verses being called 'quotations'.

Here are some of the best known quotations from the work of Robert Burns. Do you recognise any of them? You could discuss them with other people, perhaps. Or why not make a book – in class or by yourself – of some of your own favourite quotations and find out what they mean?

➠ ➠ ➠

From 'Tam o Shanter'

> But pleasures are like poppies spread:
> You seize the flow'r, its bloom is shed;
> Or like the snow falls in the river,
> A moment white – then melts for ever;
> Or like the borealis race,
> That flit ere you can point their place;
> Or like the rainbow's lovely form
> Evanishing amid the storm.

–   Do you like this part of the poem? It is in English, rather than in the Scots language. Does that sound better to you or not?
–   Do you know what the 'borealis race' is?
–   What kinds of pictures do these lines conjure up in your mind?

'Tam o Shanter' (continued)

> Nae man can tether time or tide ...

– What does 'tether' mean? What is the poet saying to us here?

❖ ❖ ❖

From 'A Man's a Man for a' that'

> The rank is but the guinea's stamp,
>   The man's the gowd for a' that.

– What do you think Robert Burns is saying here?
– Do you know what a 'guinea' is? Why should it have a stamp on it? What is meant by a 'stamp' in this poem?
– What does 'gowd' mean?

> Then let us pray that come it may
>   (As come it will for a' that),
> That Sense and Worth o'er a' the earth,
>   Shall bear the gree an a' that.
> For a' that, an a' that,
>   It's comin yet for a' that,
> That man to man, the world, o'er
>   Shall brithers be for a' that.

– *bear the gree* = to take first place
– Do you like this poem? Why do you think it would be a good thing if the poet's wish could come true?

From 'Man was made to Mourn – A Dirge'

'Man's inhumanity to man
Makes countless thousands mourn!'

– Do you know what a 'Dirge' is?
– What does 'man's inhumanity' mean?
– What sort of things would make you sad?
What sort of things do you think would make other people sad?

'O Death! the poor man's dearest friend,
The kindest and the best!'

– This is a very hard quotation for young people to understand,
because people are usually a bit afraid of death. How can death
be a 'friend'? How can death be 'kind'? What do you think?

From 'To a Mouse'

The best-laid schemes o mice an men
Gang aft agley,
An lea'e us nought but grief an pain,
For promis'd joy!

– *gang aft agley* = often go wrong
– Do you think this a true saying? Or is the poet being too sad?

❧ ❧ ❧

From 'Address to the Unco Guid'

Then gently scan your brother man,
Still gentler sister woman;
Tho they may gang a kennin wrang,
To step aside is human ...

- *kennin* = a little bit
- What do you think Robert Burns means in this quotation?
- Find out what 'Unco Guid' means.

❧ ❧ ❧

From 'To a Louse'

O wad some Power the giftie gie us
To see oursels as ithers see us!
It wad frae monie a blunder free us,
An foolish notion:
What airs in dress an gait wad lea'e us,
An ev'n devotion!

- What do you think Robert Burns is saying here?
Do you think he's right?
- Do you know what a 'louse' is?

◗ ◗ ◗

From 'Epistle to Davie, A Brother Poet'

The heart ay's the part ay
That makes us right or wrang.

– What does 'ay' mean here?
– Do you think the poet is right?

◗ ◗ ◗

From 'The Cotter's Saturday Night'

From scenes like these, old Scotia's grandeur springs,
That makes her lov'd at home, rever'd abroad:
Princes and lords are but the breath of kings,
'An honest man's the noblest work of God' …

– The scene described in this poem is of a poor family saying their prayers and reading the Bible together in their house. Do you think that reading the Bible at home should still be an important part of family life?
– What is 'old Scotia?' What does 'grandeur' mean?
– Do you think an honest man is more important than a prince or a lord?

◆◇ ◆◇ ◆◇

From 'Green grow the Rashes, O'

Auld Nature swears, the lovely dears
Her noblest work she classes, O:
Her prentice han' she try'd on man,
An then she made the lasses, O.

– What do you think the word 'Rashes' means in this title?
What does 'prentice' mean? (Hint – it sounds very like a word
most of you will know already.)
– Robert Burns is making both a joke and a serious point here.
What do you think they are?
– There are some very good points here for anyone preparing
a Reply to the Toast 'The Lassies!' during a Burns Supper
(see pages 78 to 79). What do you think they are?

◆◇ ◆◇ ◆◇

From 'A Dream'

But facts are chiels that winna ding,
An downa be disputed ...

– What do you think 'winna ding' means?
What does 'downa' mean?
– We have a modern way of saying this quotation – 'facts are
facts'. Do you think Robert's way of saying it sounds better?

LOVE POEMS

Robert Burns wrote lots of poems and songs about love. Here are three quotations from some of his poem/songs. What do you think about them?

From 'Ae Fond Kiss' (Farewell to Nancy)

Ae fond kiss, and then we sever!
Ae fareweel, and then forever!

— Do you think the people in this song are happy or sad?
Why do you think that?
— 'Ae' means 'one' – why do you think there was only one kiss?
— What does 'sever' mean?

From 'John Anderson, My Jo'

John Anderson my jo, John,
We clamb the hill thegither,
And monie a cantie day, John,
We've had wi ane anither;
Now we maun totter down, John,
And hand in hand we'll go,
And sleep thegither at the foot,
John Anderson, my jo!

- What does 'cantie' mean?
- What does Robert Burns mean by the characters of this poem/song climbing a hill together?
  Why are they 'tottering' downhill?
- Do you think this poem is about old people or young people?
- Have the couple known one another for a long time?

[Robert Burns wrote more than one version of this particular poem/song.]

From 'My Luve Is Like A Red, Red Rose'

> O, my luve's like a red, red rose,
> > That's newly sprung in June.
> O, my luve's like the melodie,
> > That's sweetly play'd in tune.

- Do you like this verse, or do you think it's a bit soppy?
  What does 'newly' mean? What is a 'melodie'?
  What does 'sweetly' mean in this poem?
- Do you know what a June rose looks like? Does it smell nice?
- Do you think the girl in the poem – Robert Burns' 'luve' – would be pleased to be compared to a rose?

Robert based this poem on an old 'ballad' – a slow and tender, often very popular song with simple words. The tune would have been written by another person, but Burns heard it and liked it and wrote words to fit the music. It appears that he did this quite a lot!

CHAPTER 5

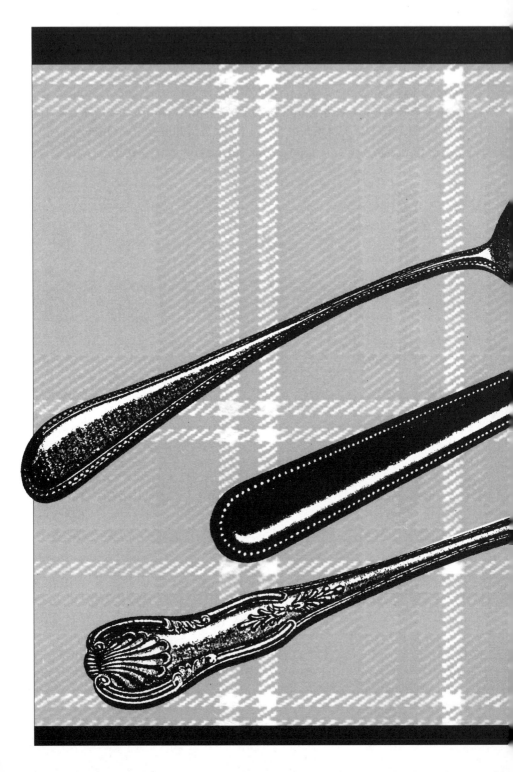

A Burns Supper
D.I.Y.

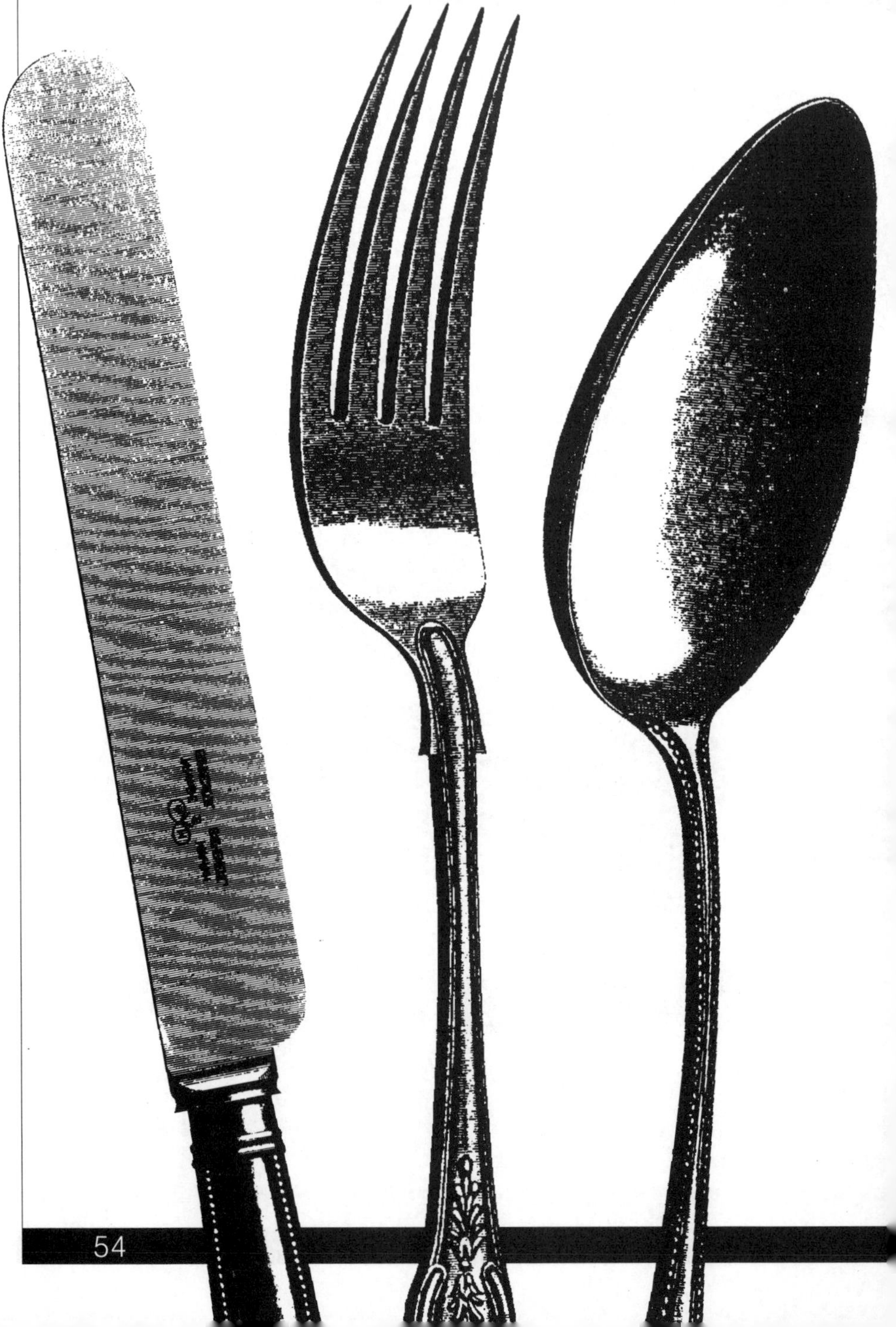

WHEN

he was a young man, Robert Burns and his friends used to meet in one another's houses, or in public houses, inns or taverns in the area where they stayed. There they enjoyed talking and arguing and singing songs.

One particular house they met in was at Tarbolton, Ayrshire. This seventeenth century thatched house can still be seen today and is in the care of the National Trust for Scotland, a charity which looks after many castles and other historic sites in this country. Robert Burns and his friends formed a debating club there in 1780.

Imagine the scene. The air is smoky with clay-pipe tobacco; the sound of quarrelling and singing fills the small room. The men sup their drinks and eat hungrily after a busy day in the fields.

What might they be eating? Well, sometimes they ate a haggis. In Robert Burns' time a haggis was a real treat. It was a special kind of food – a 'delicacy'. Nowadays we still eat haggis. Do you know what it is made of? (See page 60.)

Robert and his friends formed a club, but only men and boys could join. This was common enough in Burns' day, though today lots of people think that men-only organisations are wrong.

Because Burns and his friends were not married, they called their club the 'Tarbolton Bachelors' Club'.

Not long after Robert Burns died, people wanted to honour his memory. But how would they do this? Someone came up with a good idea – they could hold a Dinner or Supper in the same way as Burns and his friends did in their Bachelors' Club.

What form would this Dinner or Supper take?

Well, they could read Robert's poems and sing his songs.

And perhaps they could drink a 'Toast' to his memory. After all, grown-ups do that on special occasions. They take a glass of wine or whisky or lemonade or water, or any other drink, in one hand and think hard about the special person or occasion. Then they raise their glass up in front of them and say special words to fit the occasion. This is called the 'Toast' (which has nothing to do with bread!).

These words are like a salute. They are like awarding a prize to someone special.

Once the special words have been said, the person drinks from his or her glass.

After Burns died, his friends would raise their glasses and say 'Robert Burns'. Then they would take a drink. In this way they were honouring his memory.

These Suppers became more common. As the years passed, more and more people who liked the poems and songs of Robert Burns would hold special Suppers in his honour. Most of these were held on or close to the day Robert was born – the 25th of January.

At these Suppers people also ate a haggis – partly because it was a special treat in Robert's day and partly because he wrote a great poem about a haggis (see pages 64-65). It wasn't a serious poem. It was supposed to make people chuckle and laugh. And it still does that today.

We have already said that millions of people all over the world liked Robert's poems and songs, which were written down for people to read in their own languages. They too began to hold more and more Burns Suppers until thousands of Suppers came to be held each year, mostly around the 25th of January – although one or two are held in February and some even in the Summer.

There have been many famous writers in Scotland, like Sir Walter Scott, Robert Louis Stevenson, John Buchan, and many others.

There have been many famous writers in England, such as William Shakespeare, John Milton, William Wordsworth, and so on.

There have been many famous writers in other countries, like Victor Hugo in France, Mark Twain in America, and Leo Tolstoy in Russia, and lots, lots more.

Some of these writers are also remembered and honoured at special Dinners or other events when an anniversary of their death or birthday comes round, often every 25 or 50 years.

But they don't have a *special event, every year,* in *lots of countries.*

Only Robert Burns has that.

So, you see, he is a *very* special man.

It is a nice thought that every year, all over the world and at around the same time, people hold a party just to honour Robert Burns, his poems and songs.

So, here is an idea – why don't *you* organise a Burns Supper at home, or in your class or school?

It's great fun! It's not hard. Here's what should happen.

A BURNS SUPPER
PLANNING THE EVENT

Burns Suppers should be lots of fun, but everything must be planned with care. Plan your Supper a long time *before* the date chosen for the event. You will need to work out the following details:

- First of all set a date. It is best to hold your Supper or party in January or February.
- Decide where the Supper is going to be held.
- Draw up a guest list, design an invitation and send the invitations out to your guests.
- Plan a programme of events – the poems and songs you will be using and in what order they will come in the programme. There are funny bits and serious bits in a Burns Supper. Try to get a good balance.
- Organise some music to go with the event.
- Plan a menu of the kind of food and drink you want to eat at your Supper. It is nice to eat traditional Scottish food at a Burns Supper, if that is possible. And why not have a glass of Barr Irn-Bru® with your meal, or lemonade, or even water. Ask someone to give you some advice – like a teacher or parent.
- Choose someone to be the 'Chairperson'. He or she will be the 'boss'! It is up to that person to welcome the guests to the Supper and to announce the songs and poems when each point in the programme is reached.
- Choose a main speaker to talk about how wonderful a poet Robert Burns was. This is for the part of the programme called 'The Immortal Memory' (see pages 67-68). Pick other people to recite the poems you have chosen for your programme.

A BURNS SUPPER PROGRAMME

Here is a suggested order of events for your programme. This is the way a lot of people organise their Burns Suppers:

The Grace

- First of all, the Chairperson should welcome the guests with a short speech. Keep it simple!
- Then 'Grace' is said. This is a little prayer spoken before eating a meal. Most people said Grace in Robert Burns' time before starting their food and some people still do so today.

The Grace used at Burns Suppers is often called the 'Selkirk Grace'. The original version of this Grace may not have been written by Robert Burns himself, but he would have known the original well. It is written that Robert once used an English version of the Grace at the Earl of Selkirk's home at St Mary's Isle, Kirkcudbright, in south-west Scotland. That is why it is known as the 'Selkirk Grace'. Here, however, is the version used at a lot of Burns Suppers:

> Some hae meat and canna eat.
> And some wad eat that want it:
> But we hae meat and we can eat,
> And sae the Lord be thanket.

- *meat* = food
- Try to learn this Grace off by heart, but you can read it from a card if that is easier for you.

The Haggis

— Next a Haggis is carried in to your Supper as if it were part of a formal procession.

You will need to order a haggis from your butcher (or the meat counter in a supermarket) well in advance and get it cooked or heated up. You can even cook a haggis in a microwave, if you have one. **[Remember to ask an adult before you try to cook your haggis, to avoid any accidents.]**

It may not be easy to find somewhere to cook a haggis in your school, so choose something else for your meal.

The Haggis is really meant as a 'symbol'. It is a reminder to us of the life of Robert Burns and the type of food he too would have eaten over two centuries ago. So it is best to have a haggis, a real one, and one that is properly cooked.

What is a Haggis?

A haggis can look like a kind of sausage, but it is usually more like a ball in shape. It is made of ingredients like oatmeal, beef-suet, meat, onions, salt, pepper, cayenne (a spice) and marjoram (a herb) – mixed together. All these ingredients are minced, that is ground into very small pieces.

Then the minced ingredients are sewn into the stomach bag of a sheep. Don't say *yuck!* You don't have to eat the bag!

Properly cooked, haggis tastes delicious! People often eat mashed turnip and potatoes with it.

Where did the name 'Haggis' come from?

Some people say that the name 'haggis' comes from a French word 'hachis' which means 'minced meat'. (The countries of Scotland and France were close allies long ago and would have shared some of their words, fashions and foods.)

But that meaning is unlikely. Instead, the word 'haggis' probably comes from the Scots word 'hag', which means 'to chop' or 'to hack'.

★ ★ ★

Robert Burns and his friends liked eating haggis at their parties. So do we! It's fun, but it has a serious meaning too. What is the meaning of the Haggis? Well, it reminds us of the life and times of Robert Burns and how this famous poet lived.

The Procession

After your Chairperson has welcomed the guests, and before the haggis meal is eaten, you need to have a procession to bring in the Haggis. This is how to do it:

– After the Grace, the Chairperson asks everyone to stand.
– Now the procession comes in.
  It includes one person who carries a tray or plate on which the haggis is placed.
  [Remember, a sharp knife is also needed to cut the Haggis open. Please be *very* careful using a knife – it might be best to let your teacher or parents handle it and make sure it is ready for you at the main table.]

- You also need to have music to accompany the procession of people when they walk into the Supper room.
- The group of people in the procession normally walk straight from the kitchen, where all the haggis has been cooked or prepared. Or, if that is not possible, they can wait outside the door until the right time. At grown-up Burns Suppers there is usually a piper who 'pipes in' the Haggis. But you could have a fiddle to play your music, or a mouth organ, or a group of you who can sing or hum a march tune, or even a cassette player with suitable music on the tape.

Here is the order of the procession:

- The musicians or singers lead the procession.
- Behind them comes the person carrying the plate or tray with the Haggis.
- Behind the tray-carrier walks another person who has been chosen to read out the Robert Burns' poem called 'Address to a Haggis'.
- Sometimes there is another person in the procession – a character called 'Poosie Nancy' But, who is she?

When Robert stayed in the village of Mauchline, Ayrshire, one particular tavern or pub he visited was owned by a woman called Mrs Gibson or 'Poosie Nancy'. (The tavern is still there and it is still called 'Poosie Nancy's'.) Robert Burns loved going to that tavern.

But what about 'Poosie Nancy' herself? Well, the name 'Poosie' may have come from an old Scots word 'pouss' meaning 'to urge on'. Nancy was that kind of person – lively and fun-loving. She wanted people to have a good time. She welcomed them. She liked to see them happy and enjoying themselves.

In your Burns Supper procession you can have someone dressed as Poosie Nancy. It means that you are likely to have a good time too. Whoever is playing Poosie Nancy should wear a large apron and a white cotton mob-cap of the kind worn long ago. It is a bit like a large white handkerchief gathered loosely around the crown of the head, with a broad head band and a frilly edge.

And so, in comes the procession, with the audience clapping in time to the music:

- The procession stops in front of the Chairperson. Then the person who is to recite (say) the 'Address to a Haggis' – that's the proper name for this part of the programme – starts to speak.
- At the third verse of the poem, that same person picks up the knife – or is handed it – and, with a flourish, cuts the Haggis. (Or, you can wait until the end of the poem and cut it then, if you like.) You will find the poem on the next page.
- Then there is a Toast – 'The Haggis'! Look for the drink in front of you and raise the glass up. When the Chairperson says, 'Ladies and Gentlemen – The Haggis!', the guests answer, 'The Haggis!' Everyone takes a sip from their own glass.
- Then the procession marches out again. You should give the person who recited the poem, 'Address to a Haggis', a great clap or cheer as the procession marches out.
- You can now settle down for your Supper meal. That, of course, includes eating the haggis on the plate in front of you, which is cooked at the same time as the Procession Haggis, and is made up of the same ingredients.

Address to a Haggis

FAIR fa' your honest, sonsie face,
Great chieftain o the puddin'-race!
Aboon them a' ye tak your place,
    Painch, tripe, or thairm:
Weel are ye wordy o a grace
    As lang's my arm.

The groaning trencher there ye fill,
Your hurdies like a distant hill,
Your pin wad help to mend a mill
    In time o need,
While thro your pores the dews distil
    Like amber bead.

His knife see rustic Labour dight,
An cut you up wi ready slight,
Trenching your gushing entrails bright,
    Like onie ditch;
And then, O what a glorious sight,
    Warm-reekin, rich!

Then, horn for horn, they stretch an strive:
Deil tak the hindmost, on they drive,
Till a' their weel-swall'd kytes belyve
    Are bent like drums;
Then auld guidman, maist like to rive,
    'Bethankit' hums.

Is there that owre his French *ragout,*
Or *olio* that wad staw a sow,
Or *fricassee* wad mak her spew
    Wi perfect sconner,
Looks down wi sneering, scornfu view
    On sic a dinner?

Poor devil! see him owre his trash,
As feckless as a wither'd rash,
His spindle shank a guid whip-lash,
    His nieve a nit;
Thro bloody flood or field to dash,
    O how unfit!

But mark the Rustic, haggis-fed,
The trembling earth resounds his tread,
Clap in his walie nieve a blade,
    He'll make it whissle;
An legs an arms, an heads will sned,
    Like taps o thrissle.

Ye Pow'rs, wha mak mankind your care,
And dish them out their bill o fare,
Auld Scotland wants nae skinking ware
    That jaups in luggies;
But, if ye wish her gratefu prayer,
    Gie her a Haggis!

WORD LIST

sonsie	=	pleasant, cheerful
aboon	=	above
thairm	=	gut or intestine
trencher	=	a plate or platter
hurdies	=	your bottom!
dight	=	to wipe
kytes	=	bellies
belyve	=	by-and-by or soon
staw	=	to sicken
sconner	=	dislike, loathing
nieve	=	a fist
nit	=	a nut
walie	=	large
sned	=	to cut off or trim
thrissle	=	a thistle
skinking	=	watery
jaups	=	splashes
luggies	=	milk dish for porridge

– Now, after your meal, you should entertain your guests with a Burns song. Try to get everyone to sing along. What about 'Killiecrankie' (see pages 73-74)?

– Then someone should recite or read a small Burns poem – like 'To a Mouse' (see pages 16-17) or 'To a Mountain Daisy'.

The Immortal Memory

Then comes the most important part of your Burns Supper – 'The Immortal Memory'. What is this?

– Every Burns Supper should have a main speaker. He or she now gives a little talk about how wonderful a poet Robert Burns was, praising his poems and songs. Or sometimes the speaker takes just one part of Robert's life and talks about that.

At grown-up Burns Suppers, the speaker can talk for minutes, sometimes up to an hour! So you can make your talk as long or as short as you like. Five minutes is probably fine.

But remember, you must call this part of the programme 'The Immortal Memory'. 'Immortal' means 'to live forever' and 'never to be forgotten'! Why do you think people say that Robert Burns' memory – that is, the way we remember him – is 'immortal'?

– For this part of the programme – 'The Immortal Memory' – you should choose the boy or girl who will do it best to be the speaker. Listen to him or her in silence. It is nice to show good manners at a Burns Supper.

The speaker should think very hard about what he or she wants to say. Perhaps he or she could discuss the speech with a teacher or parent or friend.

– When the speech is ready, write it down in note form. The speaker may wish to read out the speech from the words in front of him or her, but it is perhaps better to learn by heart the main points of the speech and to say it without the notes. However, keep the notes handy in case the speaker forgets a point or two.

– At the end of the speech, the speaker should ask the guests to stand up. They should have a glass in their hand.

– The speaker says: 'Ladies and Gentlemen! Robert Burns – The Immortal Memory!'

– The guests reply: 'Robert Burns! The Immortal Memory!' They should hold their glasses up, sip from them, and sit down again.

– Now give the speaker a *big* cheer!

'The Immortal Memory' is indeed the most serious and important part of the Burns Supper. It is a bit like a sermon. It is a bit like a lesson in class. People learn a lot every year about Robert Burns from this part of the programme. Whereas the Toast to 'The Haggis' is good fun, the Toast to 'The Immortal Memory' is very important.

– At this point in the programme there comes another song and another poem. There can be more than one poem, if you have time – there are certainly lots to choose from.

Tam o Shanter

During the Burns Supper the poem 'Tam o Shanter' should be read or recited (see pages 27-34). Most people choose to recite it *after* 'The Immortal Memory'.

Songs

The songs of Robert Burns are loved all over the world. However, not all the songs found in the books of Robert Burns' works were written by him in the beginning. Why was this? Well, sometimes he took old songs and made changes to the original words. Or sometimes he wrote entirely new words for tunes he and his friends liked.

Here are two songs which are the favourites of lots of people. One is a gentle tune, a love song called 'The Banks o Doon'. The other song has a faster tune and you can beat time to it with your hands or feet. It tells about a battle – the battle of Killiecrankie.

The Banks o Doon

Play or sing at a moderate pace.

The Banks o Doon

YE banks and braes o bonie Doon,
    How can ye bloom sae fresh and fair?
How can ye chant, ye little birds,
    And I sae weary fu o care!
Thou'll break my heart, thou warbling bird,
    That wantons thro the flowering thorn!
Thou minds me o departed joys,
    Departed never to return.

Aft hae I rov'd by bonie Doon
    To see the rose and woodbine twine,
And ilka bird sang o its luve,
    And fondly sae did I o mine.
Wi lightsome heart I pu'd a rose,
    Fu sweet upon its thorny tree!
And my fause luver staw my rose –
    But ah! he left the thorn wi me.

WORD LIST

wantons	=	frolics, or moves in a carefree way
ilka	=	each, every
staw	=	stole

QUESTIONS

— 'The Banks o Doon' is a love song. It is a very lovely song and is very popular. It has a slow and beautiful tune (see page 70). It is a song about joy. It is also a song about sadness. Why is the singer — the girl — so full of grief? What do you think has happened to her?

— Robert Burns loved the countryside, the green fields and braes, the singing birds, the flowers. But they made the singer sad. Do you find that strange?

— The Doon is a river in Ayrshire. Can you find it on the map of Scotland?

Killiecrankie

Play or sing at a brisk pace.

Killiecrankie

'WHARE hae ye been sae braw, lad?
Whare hae ye been sae brankie, O?
Whare hae ye been sae braw, lad?
Cam ye by Killiecrankie, O?

CHORUS:
An ye had been whare I hae been,
    Ye wad na been sae cantie, O!
An ye had seen what I hae seen,
    On the braes o Killiecrankie, O!

'I faught at land, I faught at sea,
    At hame I faught my auntie, O;
But I met the Devil an Dundee,
    On the braes o Killiecrankie, O.

CHORUS:
An ye had been whare I hae been, etc.

'The bauld Pitcur fell in a furr,
    An Clavers gat a clankie, O,
Or I had fed an Athole gled,
    On the braes o Killiecrankie, O!'

CHORUS:
An ye had been whare I hae been, etc.

WORD LIST

braw	=	fine, handsome
brankie	=	spruce, finely dressed
cantie	=	lively, cheerful
furr	=	a deep furrow, or ditch
clankie	=	a knock, or blow
gled	=	a hawk

Killiecrankie – The Background

'Killiecrankie' is a song about a battle that took place on the 27th of July 1689.

On the one side were the Highlanders, led by John Graham of Claverhouse. He was also known as Viscount Dundee, hence his nickname – 'Bonnie Dundee'.

On the other side were troops mainly from the Lowlands. They were led by General Hugh Mackay of Scourie (his surname is pronounced 'Scow-ray').

The battle took place at Killiecrankie, in the district called Atholl (Athole = old spelling), in Perthshire.

The two armies were fighting over *who* should be the King of Scotland at that time. General Hugh Mackay wanted William of Orange on the throne, but John Graham of Claverhouse favoured King James VII of Scotland (also James II of England) who had fled to France at the time. He went to live at St Germaine, as a guest of King Louis XIV of France.

The Battle of Killiecrankie was the first battle to be fought by people known as 'Jacobites'. The word 'Jacobite' comes from the Latin word for 'James' – *Jacobus*. They were followers of King James VII, a Stuart King of Scotland. Like Graham of Claverhouse, they wanted the House of Stuart back on the throne. The Stuart Kings had ruled Scotland for many centuries until James VII was forced to abandon his rule over Scotland and England, leaving his son-in-law William of Orange to accept the throne in his absence.

At the end of the fighting Graham of Claverhouse's Jacobite side won the battle, but Claverhouse himself was killed during the fighting.

★ ★ ★

Robert Burns wrote only the verses of this song, and not the chorus. The story of the song 'Killiecrankie' is told from the viewpoint of one of General Mackay's defeated men. It tells how he only survived the battle because Graham of Claverhouse and another leader, called Haliburton of Pitcur, were killed, thus allowing him to escape.

The words are 'ironic'. That means they are not quite what they appear. At first sight it may seem as though the song is sympathetic to the Lowland troops under General Mackay, but in fact the Jacobites are taking the mickey when they sing it. They are crowing over their enemies. They are saying 'we won! we won!' And they are gloating too, by pretending it is one of their enemies who is singing this song which is based on an old and popular Jacobite song. 'Yes, sing away!' say the Jacobites to this enemy singer, 'but remember that you're a very lucky man to be alive – it is only because our leaders [Haliburton of Pitcur and Claverhouse] are dead that you have survived – and *we all* know that!'

And so, what Robert Burns has done here is to take an old and well-known Jacobite song and change it around a bit to make the song mean more to its audience. It is very clever.

'Killiecrankie' has a very lively tune. It is called 'An Ye had been whare I hae been'. Lots of folk groups sing this song. You might be able to find it on a record or a cassette or a compact disc.

The Lassies

There is one other Toast every Burns Supper must have. It is called 'The Lassies!'

– One person (it must be a boy or a man) is chosen before the event to make a short speech about girls and women. It should be a nice speech, in praise of girls and women – but it should be lighthearted too. It is meant to be good fun!

    Have a practice go! Try to think up some jokes or funny things about girls in your class, or women that you know – even your teachers. But be *kind* about it. No nasty jokes. No cruel jokes. No dirty jokes. Just make it good fun.

    Think hard about all the girls in your class. Go on, pull their legs a bit! If you are asked to do the Toast – 'The Lassies' – ask your friends in class to help you with ideas. And remember, it need not be a long Toast.

– When the person chosen to make this speech has finished, he must ask only the boys and men to stand up again. He should raise his glass and make a Toast to the girls, saying: 'Gentlemen – The Lassies!'
– The boys and men stand and say: 'The Lassies!'
Then they take a sip of their drink.
– The guests should then clap this speaker for giving such a funny speech.

The Reply

- Now the girls get their revenge. One girl, chosen before the event, is called upon to give a Reply speech. She can get her own back on the boys.
- The girl giving 'The Reply' could ask her friends for help when making up her speech. What do you know about the boys in your class? Try to prepare a funny Reply. Make jokes! Pull the boys' legs this time. Make jokes about boys in general. Ask a teacher or your parents to help. They'll know lots of good jokes. You can borrow some of these.

    Your reply need not be long. A few minutes will do. But do try to get your own back.
- This speech is known as The Reply to 'The Lassies'. The girl giving this Reply should also get lots of applause from the guests when she has finished.

Auld Lang Syne

All Burns Suppers should end with the singing of the song 'Auld Lang Syne'. This song is about remembering old friendships. It is about being happy at having had a good time. The song also means that people hope to meet again and be happy once more.

'Auld Lang Syne' is a famous song and is sung all over the world.

Some people pronounce 'syne' as 'zyne' – which is wrong. It should be 'syne'.

Nearly everyone today sings 'Auld Lang Syne' in a different way to the song composed by Robert Burns all those centuries ago. It is good to get it right. Here is Robert's own version. If it is too long for a class or house Burns Supper, then you can leave out some of the verses.

Auld Lang Syne

Play or sing at a steady pace.

Auld Lang Syne

Should auld acquaintance be forgot,
And never brought to mind?
Should auld acquaintance be forgot,
And auld lang syne?

CHORUS:
For auld lang syne, my jo,
For auld lang syne,
We'll tak a cup o kindness yet,
For auld lang syne!

And surely ye'll be your pint-stowp,
And surely I'll be mine,
And we'll tak a cup o kindness yet,
For auld lang syne!

CHORUS:
For auld lang syne, my jo, etc.

We twa hae run about the braes,
And pou'd the gowans fine,
But we've wander'd mony a weary fit,
Sin auld lang syne.

CHORUS:
For auld lang syne, my jo, etc.

We twa hae paidl'd in the burn
    Frae morning sun till dine,
But seas between us braid hae roar'd
    Sin auld lang syne.

    CHORUS:
    For auld lang syne, my jo, etc.

And there's a hand my trusty fiere,
    And gie's a hand o thine,
And we'll tak a right guid-willie waught,
    For auld lang syne.

    CHORUS:
    For auld lang syne, my jo, etc.

WORD LIST

auld lang syne	=	old long ago
my jo	=	my dear, my darling
pint-stowp	=	a tankard, or drinking vessel
pou'd	=	pulled
gowans	=	daisies
dine	=	dinner-time
fiere	=	a companion
guid-willie waught	=	a goodwill drink, a hearty draught

The Running Order of a Burns Supper

Sometimes people are not sure in what order a Burns Supper should run. Grown-up Burns Suppers can differ. Here is a possible programme for you:

1 Chairperson's Welcome.
2 Entry of the Haggis and the 'Address to the Haggis'.
3 Grace and the Meal –
   (sometimes the Grace is said *before* the Haggis is brought in).
4 A Burns Song or Poem.
5 'The Immortal Memory'.
6 A Burns Song or Poem.
7 A reading of 'Tam o Shanter' –
   (sometimes it is read before 'The Immortal Memory').
8 The Toast to 'The Lassies'.
9 The Reply to 'The Lassies'.
10 'Auld Lang Syne'.

Some grown-up Burns Suppers have more songs in them. Others have less. Some have extra Toast-speeches like 'To Scotland!', or to the village, town or city where the Supper is being held, or to the organisation which is holding the Supper.

You might like to have an extra Toast – 'To our School!' Indeed, you can make all sorts of changes, if you like. The *important* thing is that you *enjoy* the event. The best Burns Suppers are lots of fun, but good manners are expected and you must remember that the Supper has a serious side to it as well – the memory of Robert Burns.

A shorter Burns Supper programme, perhaps for a Supper held during the day in your classroom, might be as follows:

1　Chairperson's Welcome.
2　The 'Address to the Haggis'.
3　Grace and Meal.
4　A Burns Song or Poem.
5　'The Immortal Memory'.
6　A reading of 'Tam o Shanter' –
　　(or parts of it if you don't have a lot of time).
7　The Toast to 'The Lassies'.
8　The Reply to 'The Lassies'.
9　'Auld Lang Syne'.

Publications on ROBERT BURNS referred to in this book include:

- Dr James A Mackay (editor): *The Complete Poetical Works of Robert Burns 1759-1796* (Bicentenary edition, completely revised), published by Alloway Publishing, Darvel, Ayrshire, 1993.
- William Scott Douglas (editor): *The Kilmarnock Edition of the Poetical Works of Robert Burns* (verbatim copy), 1876.
- William Scott Douglas (editor): *The Poetical Works of Robert Burns – Posthumous Publications*, 1876.
- James Barke (editor): *Poems and Songs of Robert Burns*, 1955.

Also referred to:

- Mairi Robinson (editor-in-chief): *The Concise Scots Dictionary*, originally published by Aberdeen University Press, 1985.

Further reading about ROBERT BURNS for children:

- Irving Miller (compiler): *Burns for Bairns*, published by Alloway Publishing, Darvel, Ayrshire.
  'A selection of poems or extracts from poems by ROBERT BURNS suitable for reading or recitation by children of all ages, whether in competitions, festivals or simply for their own enjoyment ... '

References

The Dumyat Trilogy
by Rennie McOwan

LIGHT ON DUMYAT,
THE WHITE STAG ADVENTURE
and
THE DAY THE MOUNTAIN MOVED

'At first, the light seemed to Gavin like a shooting star that had shot across the hill of Dumyat and disappeared …. Then he saw it again, differently … it looked as if someone had opened the door of a lighted room, and closed it again – quickly. But a room on a hill was impossible – wasn't it? Tomorrow, he would climb Dumyat and find out.'

In the third volume – *The Day the Mountain Moved* – Gavin and his friends, fresh from *Light on Dumyat* and *The White Stag Adventure*, go back in time to face the 'good' and 'bad' figures of Scottish Celtic mythology, like Ossian and Deirdre of the Sorrows.

Educational and very exciting. A popular children's adventure series for 7-12 year olds.

Light on Dumyat was chosen for a primary schools conference at Stirling University; *The White Stag Adventure* was broadcast by BBC for schools; and *The Day the Mountain Moved* reached the Scottish Top Ten Books. All three books are used in Scottish schools.

Children's Books
by **Rennie McOwan**